"Reading Carol Bialock's poems, I forget to doubt and critique and meddle and complain. Here is a spiritual poetry that offers the reader vivid, dynamic, immediate, ecstatic experience on a human scale. 'Dizzy with love and light,' this book is a delight."

Katie Peterson
author of *A Piece of Good News*

"Carol Bialock's work hums in wise praise of a world hemmed in mystery and wildness. Brilliant and luminous, each poem burns with a quiet, interior light."

Gina Ochsner
author of *The Hidden Letters of Velta B.*

"'All you need is a little courage' Carol Bialock declares, and then takes us through image and rhythm on a "trip to the edge of the world" where we encounter sacred mysteries, the heart of the poet, and our own surprising wholeness. This work is lighthearted and holy, whimsical and profound—the fruit of a life spent watching for wonder, the gift of a soul in love with the world."

Bethany Lee
author of *The Breath Between*

"Honestly, the poetry of Carol Bialock is stunning! Her ability to communicate inner states, universal truths, and spiritual depth is unparalleled. What a loss that the world did not discover her earlier! But it is not too late!"

Richard Rohr, OFM
Founder of the Center for
Action and Contemplation

"Carol Bialock's Coral Castles is a wide and generous door into poetry and joy. These poems offer us a merging of forces that are tangible and full of delight: here we find bone meeting soul, I journeying to We, and the seen fearlessly greeting the unseen. 'Go sane,' the poems tell us, 'You are the whole, not part...Come home to being world / and galaxy / and universe.' This is a book of love and God in which poet and poem also fuse, bursting into bloom. I want to give it to everyone I know, saying, 'Look and see!'"

Annie Lighthart
author of *Iron String and Lantern*

"Carol Bialock's heart is a 'huge and lovely land' filled with poems of invitation to the available communion in every moment. They affirm that God is irresistibly, mysteriously afoot. Sister Carol is not afraid of paradox or the embodied wild experience of the greatest, fierce and Sacred Adventure. She asks us to 'let the true Gods out' and to know 'we have been in heaven all our lives.' She is a loving companion whispering to us *look, listen, touch, right here now, do you love this world? All you need is a little courage, a dash of daring.*

Take the invitation, read these poems, walk this mystic's path, join this wise woman awhile."

Peg Edera
author of *Love Is Deeper than Distance*

Coral Castles

Carol Bialock, RSCJ

Drawings by Christa,
Raymond, and Jere Grimm

Coral Castles

Fernwood Press
Newberg, Oregon
www.fernwoodpress.com

Printed in the United States of America

Cover and interior layout and design: Mareesa Fawver Moss

Drawings by Christa, Raymond, and Jere Grimm

Cover art: "Out Across the Bay" by Christa Grimm

ISBN 978-1-59498-060-2

To my father, Harry Louis Bialock, who gave me my love of poetry and encouraged the poet in me.

Contents

Woman Power

And must I, being woman, hide my breasts?
Or may I, like the wise Africans, unveil them
and walk queenly among you,
owning the pearl,
carrying lightly my diamonds?
I walk tall, needing no crown.

Do not be afraid, then. Touch me with your eyes.
Why do you tremble on the slope of this mountain,
your fingers flooded with awe?
It is true, you are not far from mystery in this place.
It is well that you kneel before you look.

And when my child gropes blindly, weeping,
must I hide the transcendent transaction
as if to suckle were a shameful thing?
Can't you bear the beauty yet?
Or does the eye fear essences
and shade itself against infinity
in this infant god?

No, I shall be kind. The glare of my breasts is too much
for you to endure.
I must hide them, after all,
lest this simple proof of a merciful Godhead blind you,
and you blame me the rest of your days for letting you
        stare at the sun.

Breathing Underwater

I built my house by the sea.
Not on the sand, mind you.
Not on the shifting sand.
And I built it of rock.
A strong house.
By a strong sea.
And we got well acquainted, the sea and I.
Good neighbors.
Not that we spoke much.
We met in silences.
Respectful, keeping our distance,
but looking our thoughts across the fence of sand.
Always, the fence of sand our barrier;
always the sand between.

And then one day
(I still don't know how it happened), but the sea came.
Without warning.
Without welcome, even.
Not sudden and swift, but sifting across the sand like wine.
Less like the flow of water than the flow of blood.
Slow, but coming.
Slow, but flowing like an open wound.
And I thought of flight and I thought of drowning and I
    thought of death.

And while I thought the sea crept higher, till it reached my
   door.

I knew, then, there was neither flight nor death nor drowning.
That when the sea comes calling you stop being good
   neighbors,
Well-acquainted, friendly-from-a-distance neighbors.
And you give your house for a coral castle,
and you learn to breathe underwater.

To Hera

How was it
when a queen walked between courtiers
toward her throne?
The rustle of satin and silk,
the dignity of it,
her head held high
while her subjects' eyes scarcely dared look up
to gaze upon her majesty.

And what of this day in July
walking between wildflowers,
yellow, heads high,
making a path for me by the sea?
The radiant summer light,
the surf's applause,
the lizard and rabbit escorting me down the path.

Am I more or less of a queen?
My heart knows,
and I will never tell the secret.

(Point Lobos, CA 7-6-91)

The Unvisited Lands

Go to those unvisited lands.
Have your passport ready.
Cross the frontier.

You won't need baggage.
Test the soil.
Taste the water.

All you need is a little courage
a dash of daring

to go into those
unexplored vistas of your mind
to visit the too-virgin places in your heart.

On Buddha's Birthday

On Buddha's birthday, how do you celebrate?
A bit of suffering stoically borne?
A sitting session, eyes half closed?
A walk around the Bodhi tree?

Ask your own inner Buddha.

Heap up your life's experience,
sift it,
till the fine flour of wisdom covers you,
and you're ready to be baked in the Eightfold Path.

The Ultimate Sin

Give up your separateness.
For whom does the bell toll?
It tolls for you.
Who is crowned queen?
You are—and beggar, fool, and clown.
That is the sin: to be only your puny self
when you are really world and godhead.

Give up vanity, yes, and lies and pride.
Give up judging (the one you judge is yourself).
But above all, renounce being many, multitude, and mad.
Go sane.
You are the whole, not part;
the entire, not the piece.
Come home to being world
and galaxy
and universe.

I beg you,
sacrifice non-being,
the illusion of being only you.
Be what you are:
be all.
I beg of you, stop sinning:
give up your separateness.

Playing with Om

If you play around with "OM" long enough
you'll get more than your fingers scorched.

In fact, you may end up with everything, inside and
    outside, burned.

And if you keep juggling with it long enough,
all that may be left of you are
the ashes of infinite gratitude.

Truth

I tried to understand truth,
take hold, dust off, dissect, classify, label.
But before I could find its genetic code,
before I could take the trophy, triumphant,

the irresistibly real pinned me down,
held me close
and fed me at its breast.

That's how I learned to
keep silent,
drink deep.

My Way

My way makes a trail in the water
like the swan, my tiny velvet trail in time.

My way is my breath, that falls and rises,
a simple aliveness, as of unseen air,
the bottom line of life.

My way fits like skin,
a comfortable casing for the bones,
as a home has walls,
as a temple hides its prize.

I kneel within the mystery of myself
and breathe my thank you for what is.

Let the Small Gods Die

Let the small gods die
and fall back, heavy.
Sing requiem for what was.

Let the true gods out.
Pull back the curtains on opening night:
The awesome lightness we fear,
the blessing of being.

I Sleep at Home

Now I need travel no more.
That's the adventure of autumn:
the simple dance of life.
Ducks breasting the water,
a birch leaning into light.
I journey with the sun for now,
with no need for wings.
No plane rises so bright,
nor sets so softly.
I sleep at home,
and rise to look at God.

I Am of Those Who Go Down

I am of those who go down
for wisdom.
Wisdom is won through descent.
And revelation in things of earth.

Air is a teacher,
fire and water are wise,
but earth is my mentor.
I have come down to learn,
a wise descent,
a sitting at the feet of every one and every thing.

Adoration

Adoration is a bone and gut event;
It clutches you, so the knee
    is forced to bend.
It grabs you by the throat; you cannot speak.
All that is left to you is worship.

Confessions

When I come to you for pardon—
the frightened chick under the hen's wide wing,
the prodigal aching for the arms of mercy,
the penitent learning to sing—
I step into an ocean of release,
I feel the pull of your relentless mercy,
and, in the tide of your compassion, peace.

There will be, then, only the
        wordless kiss of lovers,
no need for words, knowing
        this heart can hear,
knowing I can unveil before you,
knowing a spacious freedom
        from all fear.

Inebriation

I am roses climbing around
the arbor of you,
fruit hanging from your branches,
wine from your deep cellars.

All of me,
all of me
is inebriation.

American Mystic

After you know it's all a dance
and the light is everywhere,
after the vision of the sparks on the dung-heap,
what's next, American?
What's the new wilderness to conquer,
the new challenge for your forceps?
what do you do with fullness and completion
when you were born in the USA?
What's over the horizon
when even manure is luminous?

When You Speak I Hear You

When you speak I hear you
and when you whisper the wind carries you
and the volleyball of words
is a new-found game we play together.

Today I Was a Little More Deliberate.

Today I was a little more deliberate.
I breathed into bitterness.
I was spacious inside.
I listened.
So I heard the turtle expanding in her shell;
I felt the earthworm and the lily bulb embrace,
waiting for spring.

On Being Loved

You've loved me in many ways, my God,
now, after sixty summers I know your treats:
tales a sunrise tells;
the easy silence of friendship;
and, in ultimate kindness,
death's shattering of shells.

But your tricks, now:
how compassion is squeezed from the lemon of pain;
how many winters it takes a mind to wisdom;
how you seduce with one white rose,
then spurn and trample and snub;
how your breath on the neck is hot and cold,
nothing lukewarm;
how you knock politely for years,
then suddenly tear down fences, gates, and doors
to grasp the heart like a trophy.

Now that I'm old,
mercy, my Lord.
and do not change your ways.
I want your unexpected fierceness of love
to the end of my days.

All the Years of Breaking Through the Soil

All the years of breaking through the soil,
gasping for growth,
straining to height and aroma and juice,
heavy with effort,
sweating it.

And when the glory came
and I breathed free and opened full,
strange how only then did I know
it was all gift.
I hadn't
done anything.

It was sun and rain and earth and air,
I had only to rest in
light, water, soil,
only trust and surrender
only be still
to flower into beauty.

Old Feet, Young Heart

Though my feet are too old to whirl
like the dervishes of old,
my heart is young enough to circle
round the Sun of you,
to dance one-pointedly,
to go nowhere,
dizzy with love and light.

On Eating

This is a poem about the body,
and the body at the table,
and the table as an altar,
and the body as priest,
and the prayers at the altar,
and the offering a delight,
and going in, yes, in, to the altar of God,
and the food going in to the inmost shrine,
and meeting the god there.
Oh God! meeting you there
in the food
at the table
in the inmost shrine.

Just Name Your Price

I will stand on the busiest corner of Manhattan
and shout: "Poetry for sale!"

And what a surprise
if a few stragglers say
"Just name your price.
We are so very,
so exceedingly,
so desperately
hungry!"

Poetry Divides My Life

Poetry divides my life in phases:
there were the years of reading it.
There were the years of writing it.
There were the years of living it.
And now, perhaps, the years of being it.

The One-time Show

When I stand by the sea
a long line of poets stands behind me
and they say, "Don't miss that wave!
It will never happen again in exactly the same way;
it's a one-time show!"

So I bow to Heraclitus,
and to the boy and his dog making holes in the sand,
and to the fragile landscape of sunbathers,
and to the sandcastle makers,
and to the lovers,
and to the beachcombers,
and to the picnicking families
and to the tidal wave of time
that sweeps it all away.

It's Like This

Desperate, I latch onto words.
"It's like this," and I explain God and the universe.
And all the while something pulses within,
laughs silently, and pities me.

Be What You Are

What jolts me alive is a voice
that speaks to my deafness.

This morning, from seven centuries back,
Hafiz, the Persian poet, said,

"Start seeing everything as God."
And be what you've always known you are:
    a poet.

Trickster

God always has a chess game going,
or a poker tournament.
What a trickster!
What a Clever Guy!

Be a believer in jokes,
especially the cosmic one,
the egg that gets laid daily.

You never know an egg's secret
until it breaks open;
so whether it's a chick or an elephant
doesn't matter.

Surpriser! That's who you are!
The Sneaky One who keeps us guessing,
the Joker who keeps turning up,
shaking us awake!

So Many Months

Since the voice of my soul spoke out
and woke up the world.

Now fly into the sun again,
get your wings burnt
and fall, like Icarus,
      with a living word.

A Poet Lets the Secret Out

A poet lets the secret out.
Talk about blabber-mouth!
The most intimate whisperings of God
get flaunted in the marketplace.

"This is for you," says God on the nuptial bed.
And it ends up at a poetry reading at Kepler's.
"I trust you," says God.
And next minute it's on the internet.

Strutting Around

So let words tumble out as they will,
and not dress decently for the streets
if they choose not to, but take on a life of their own,
jumbling and grumbling and tumbling and bumbling
together, till they say what they want to say in ways
not said before.

Now they are free to strut and dance across the page,
or stutter shamelessly, or turn pink with shame, but they're
out, and after a long silence they're ballooning up
for a free ride on the uncensored pages of the sky.

The Vast Silence

Children line up on the shore and watch the waves come in,
and clap when a big one makes a splash of spume
and dig big toes into the waves of sand, and laugh.
Then they look at the horizon.
Everywhere, water.
Everywhere, an incredible vastness.
And their laughter ends in wonder,
and they are caught in a vast silence.

The older ones lie on their backs and paddle,
and the waves carry them out from the shore.
They find the water holds them up.
They find they are carried where the current wills.
They believe in water; they trust the waves.
But they, too, of a sudden look:
the horizon is endless.
And they, too, are caught in a vast silence.

The old are carried out by the waves toward the horizon.
They look at the shore and wave,
and wave again, and smile.
And then they slip across the horizon,
swallowed up in the unknown.
And from the shore the others look, and wonder,
and are caught up in a vast silence.

Stand on the shore all day and into the night, and look.
There's nothing, no, there's nothing more mysterious.
There's nothing that's more like God:
the vast, the holy, the merciful silence of God.

Lofty Pretensions

What Chagall did with his painting
I want to do with my poems:
send words flying above the city,
taking crazy flight,
verses soaring, adjectives cruising,
all so natural
you're sure it must be Christmas Day.

"Nor Ever Chaste Except You Ravish Me"

Mine was a quiet house, carefully constructed,
with a certain aura of a holy site where pilgrims met
        and where the wise gave counsel,
where clowns on bright walls touched the human
    chord.
People laughed easily there, and prayed.
The opposites in happy tension played,
and who went in and out sensed pleasing power.
Even the bric-a-brac was congruent and clean.

So when I noted the crack in the floor
and saw that tree erupting,
thrusting its way through the foundations,
        up through the middle of my living room,
        toward attic and beyond toward stars,
I could only stare.

They were bare bones of a white birch stripped down
        for winter,
and their breaking through ended the cycle of my
    ordered autumn days,
shattered the sanctuary silence of my house.
The clowns
frowned,
the bric-a-brac broke
and my neat world was violated with the suddenness of
        rape.

So, this is reality, I thought.

The last rational bastions fall,
and life moves in, violent and fertile.

The birch's limbs bore holes into my closets, cabinets
        and files,
smash my chaste bed for firewood,
sweep me into cupped arms
        and rock me back to life.

The walls of my house fall down.
No house. No walls.
Only the now of the birch and I.
In its bare bark I feel all nature pulsing
and I am borne where life will take me,
with no defense against reality.
Where that white birch goes, there go I,
though we not move for half a thousand years.

Resolution

I will not let the angel of joy
flood my soul in vain
I will not let darkness
be victorious.
When fear tightens its noose,
constricts the heart,
clogs the mind,
I will go to the Man of light
who has always befriended me
and breathe deep
in the release
of His embrace.

Give Up

Give up the stressful pursuit,
abandon the furrowed brow,
learn that at the round table of the world
the sacred is the bread you break and share *now*.

Peacocks in Springtime

In spring you need a peacock feather,
like the Jain people,
to sweep a path of reverence before you,
lest you harm a living being.

And you need to take the peacock
out of your heart,
so you'll know you're just one
among the dazzling.

When will the peacock in me
become all feather
to clear a path
before the Coming One?

Wake Up Call

There's no such thing as future tense
with God.
It's all right now:
bliss and bedevilment.

And devil's the biggest myth of all;
Heaven is all there really is,
and stubbornness that doesn't know
we're there.

We fabricate the problems, but they're all
as fragile as a spider's web:
one sweep of reality and they're gone.

The real's the steadfast sun.
The real's the immense and prodigal waters
under the illusory waves.

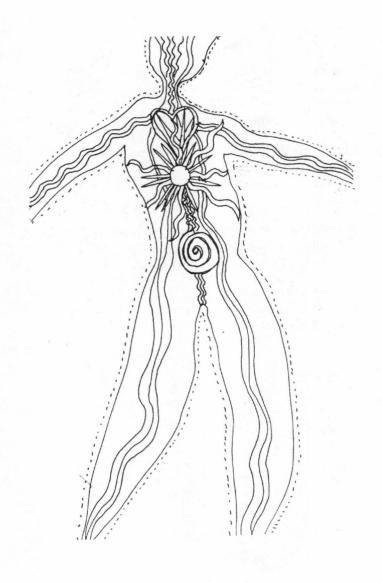

The Ostinato Song

So everything is radiance
and everything is light.
the shining of the simple
waltzes through the night.

The brashness of the sunshine,
the dimple on the moon,
all the great dichotomies
sing a simple tune.

"Good" and "evil" disappear,
gone are "right" and "wrong,"
till at last we finally hear
that ostinato song:

"There's nothing but the radiance,
there's nothing but the bright,
and what we called the darkness
is waltzing with the light."

Arrived Eyes

"Arrived eyes":
going nowhere
because they're already there.
They're a dead giveaway
of one who's been tamed.

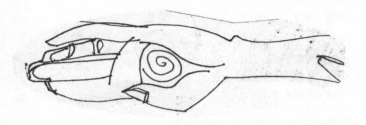

The Beatitudes

That map of happiness you gave me
    is the wedding bouquet I tossed a bit carelessly
the day after the nuptials.

I take it now,
    all eight blossoms.
They're blossoming in my heart:
    the meek, the merciful,
    the hungry, the mourners,
    the peaceful, the pure,
    the persecuted
after 50 years,
I am the happy, blessed one.

The Strange Way

Sanity is not the way.
Give yourself over to foolishness,
To the delicious business of the crazy.
Be strange. Go the crooked way
to the straight kingdom,
and you will find him.
He is hiding in a dark corner,
cast aside with his crazy friends,
throwing a party in some forgotten dungeon.
When you find him, join the celebration.

The Admirer

I admire the singer of songs
and the chanter of voices,
and I admire the listener
whose heart keeps rhythm.
And I admire the holder of the brush
whose stroke on the canvas is sure
and I admire the awed beholder
who knows how to praise.
And most of all I admire the holy ones,
those who have been supple under a sure hand
and done a work greater than themselves.

Scripture

(after a yoga class with Christa)

Body is revelation,
Holy Scriptures.

Tree, my spine, is genealogy.
I climb it, contemplating
the psalm of my voice.
The genesis of nails.
The apocalyptic entrance and exit of food.
The apostolic filters of my heartbeat,
the gospel truth of blood.

The books of my bones are historical,
and hands and feet prophecy,
lungs are spirit,
eyes and ears the Song of Songs.

May I reverently read these Scriptures,
may I never tire of this book of life.

See-saw Moment

Once upon a see-saw moment
when the Breath blew strong
and red hats turned wise,
the angel of the Lord declared
    unto a Mary-lover,
unto a lover of the poor:
and a forgotten continent
brought forth a new Peter,
lightly holding the keys
of an ever-new kingdom.

Fine Tuning

God has fine-tuned me.
I take no credit.
The piano is a silent piece of wood
until the master hand
tames strings and keys to sound together.

The Hundredth Name

Perhaps all that's left is to know
what Islam has always known:
the hundredth name of God is unknowable.

After you've memorized
the ninety-nine beautiful names
you fall on your knees and keep silence.

For the hundredth name is the Great Silence
when even angels hold in their hosannas
and even God keeps Sabbath in the silence of the Name.

Enoughness

Where is humility?
Somewhere sitting on the ground in a circle of light;
or at home base, after the perilous run
hoarding homeness.
It's holding fast for isness,
resting in enoughness,
not pining for Atlantic
when the whole Pacific is yours.

Web-making

A fine tough thread goes out from me
to every one and every thing.
I am a spider weaving webs,
and one who weaves must learn to sing
of ecstasy and anguish both
for suffering is love's own plight.

And whether love comes back to me
across that thread it matters not;
detachment's not in cutting loose
but rather binding threads more tight.

Water God

Seven years you have pounded my shore,
water God.
And I have sent your waves careening,
my rocks throw you in splitting spray
back to your ocean bed.

Today you court me again,
and my rock heart breaks in a thousand pebbles
at your touch,
and my shoreline opens to you unabashed,
waiting the onslaught of your love.

Trip to the Edge of the World

Going to the edge of the world
is something I don't plan for.
I don't measure my strength
or plot out the journey.
I just sometimes find myself there,
and hold tight to the hand that brought me,
lest I fall off.

The view is breathtaking.
I breathe deep.
All I can tell you is
there is no better place to be.

Another Country

He came.
There had been no gilt-edged invitation,
no pleading for His presence.
Love just wanted to drop in,
to surprise, as when He came
through locked doors.
His presence was comfortable,
needing no whys or wherefores,
and when He left,
an odor remained in the room,
proof of some other country.

Nothing Is More Like God Than the Ocean

Nothing is more like God than the ocean.
See, she offers her breast in every wave
her milk foams at its crest,
each wave an endless offering of nurture.

And the depths are her womb.
All things are born of water,
the ten thousand things rise from the sea.

She is the great Always-Pregnant one,
Always-Birthing, Always-Mother.

What Dries Our Tears

It's the day before catastrophe,
a perfect day, scrubbed with afternoon light,
purified for the party.

The revelers will remember this
when tomorrow's sun is black
under the rain of death.

How quickly life shifts from weal to woe,
and all our platitudes explode beneath us.

Then, on the third day,
the sun erupts from bowels of earth
and dries our tears.

Dark Fortress

She sits in front of the TV at the Family Justice Center,
all 200 pounds of her.
Rolls and rolls of brown flesh, a cocoon of flesh,
a defense, a formidable barrier against blows, against
   beatings.
She is Sorrow
She is Survival
She is a Great Brown Fortress
holding Life

The Chosen One

"When you give a banquet,"
my friend said,
"Invite the poor, the halt, the blind."
For years, these words were mystery,
a future vision,
an all-too-elusive dream.

Now, suddenly, I know
they are no longer dream,
but fact not vision,
but reality:
that I've been given
to set the table
and sit down
and have that fellowship.

Sometimes your crippled friends choose you
and you know you are
the chosen one.

The Golden Woman

Shall I tell you about the golden woman who danced in my
    dream?
Who whirled like a dervish in an effortless wind of delight,
in an ecstasy of love,
then stopped, unmoving,
as if the whirling and the stillness were one,
as if the repose, too, were dancing—
then whirled again?

Or shall I keep it secret, so that no one knows
who my night-time self is free to be?
So that no one suspects that under these rags I am radiant,
so that no one can guess that the plodding prose of my
daytime self
is a luminous rapture of rhyme in the dark of the night.

Absorber of Toxins

As I was leaving Super Cuts she came in, asking for
   a wash and cut, and we recognized each other,
   though we had never met. She told me about
   reaching an age when you're free enough within
   to absorb the toxins and move on, having purified
   the air around you. (No one need know it: you're
   just the laundry lady, or the porter at the door, or
   the preschool teacher, or the professor of physics,
   but your underground task, hidden even from you,
   is to be the Absorber of Toxins, the Purifier of Air.)
   She shared that insight and we parted. Only now,
   tonight, do I recognize she did just that for me,
   lifting me for a moment into amazing air.

On Call in a Hospital

When I'm called in to mourn with you,
whom I have never seen before;
when I touch your life at a turning point
and you explode in tears and anger
and reviling of God,
I am the rock against which you buffet and pound.
"It's not fair!"... "I don't understand!"
"Why?" ... "I'm being punished!"
I just stay steady in my granite strength.

I will not try to give you answers I know nothing of.
But, stranger, know this:
my heart has shattered into tears for you
and all this granite bleeds.

Plea to an Elder

It seems that what you learned of gymnastics as a
    child is useful for old age. The years of standing
    on your head are bearing fruit, and you're seeing
    the world right side up now. Backbends, it seems,
    have limbered you up for humility. Flip-flops have
    tumbled you into non-violence. Maybe making
    oneself into a pretzel is the only way to become food
    at the banquet table.

Please, teach me the gymnastics you've practiced all
    these years. I, too, want to be just God's fool.

Conversation: Young Woman/Old Woman

She said she swims in God.
"It's like swimming."
I held my tongue.

I wanted to tell her about floundering,
about drowning,
about arid autumns, and all the waterless ways.

But you cannot tell a summer swimmer
about December ice;

nor how, in the spring of her elder years
the pool where she swam in her youth
will be all the world's oceans wide.

The Finding of a Friend

So what is the finding of a friend
but the gradual peeling of an orange—
the tough rind begins to yield,
and the rich, juicy fruit drips in your hands,
and you taste sweetness
that quenches a life-thirst.

Prodigal Overshadowing

Ian was a torch across the threshold of my life,
the kindly light of one who judges not.
His was the stripped-down goodness of seeds,
protector of the future.
And I, for whom the masculine has always been a
    mystery,
understood at last its engendering power,
and its prodigal overshadowing, as on that first day
when Spirit hovered over the dark waters.

Enough

What is is enough.
Enough for breathing
enough food
enough drink
and enough to share with a friend.

The Longest Journey

We start alone. Uniqueness draws its breath
we burst triumphant into being, ego supreme,
each little queen sucks at her mother's breast, content.

Wit against wit we struggle to outshine.
School's one long test to see who wins.
We pyramid up; we climb the mountain of success.

And there, on top, we shiver. Aloneness hurts.
The view's fantastic, but with no one there to share
we turn to ice.

Perhaps the mountain is illusion
and level ground is where we best hold hands.
Maybe the magic's in the circle,
and everything that's blessed is plural.
The longest journey is from "I" to "we."

For Claire at 99

At 99 you are ageless,
you have moved into no-time,
older than the moon,
younger than sunshine.
Agelessness has set in like a halo.
You are, even now, a relic
    from the sea of life.
You ready yourself for exploration of
    a longed-for land
and cast anchor on a shore the
    young know nothing of.

The Hindus Knew It

The Hindus knew it:
if you kindle with prayer the heart chakra—
that great spinning central wheel of energy—
the rest of you
takes fire.

But perhaps they did not know
that friendship, too,
is a match that sets that central chakra whirling
and makes the whole of you
take flame.

I Used to Think Heaven Was Future

Suddenly I knew,
when we stood in a circle
holding hands;
suddenly I knew,
that because of the circle,
because of friendship,
because of love—
yes, and because of the brokenness,
and the need—
I have been
in heaven
all
my life.

Water Wedding

The woman in me, lake-like, looks to the mountain.
"Marry me, mountain," she says.
And the man in the mountain stands firmly planted.
"I can't," he says to the lake below.
"I am busy about many things."
The woman smiles up. She mirrors his majesty.
She is silent and deep.
She waits.
She knows she will entice him to a water wedding.

Leapfrogging

A frog leaped into my poem today.
"Kaploosh" in the water, and
"squish" onto land,
and back
and forth.

I did not know he was leapfrogging me into humanity,
that he was the humorous missing link
between water and earth in me,
making it all right to be woman,
to have a croaking good time
in both hemispheres.

So when I renew my baptismal vow this Easter
I just might throw a frog-party
to celebrate my newfound friendship with me.

The Veil Between

We breathe their bones
and their anointed bodies linger
    at our feet,
flame out in flowers,
grow tall in trees
and throw their vines around our homes.
They love us still:
the veil between us is thin.

I Embrace the World this Morning,

I embrace the world this morning,
hold her in my arms a long moment
and decide never to let her go,
never to return to safety,
never to say, "It's none of my business."
It is.

Maybe there should be a ritual
when we come of age,
when we're old enough to respond,
"I do,"
to the most crucial question:
"Do you love this world?"

Perhaps that will be the final question:
"Have you truly, deeply, faithfully
loved this world?"

Widening the Door

Does the heart have a narrow door?
Will it allow in just one more
of every beast and flower and bird
and every song it has ever heard?

Just one more child, just one more flower,
one more relinquishing of power
to that sane and sacred foolishness
of living by inclusiveness?

Does the heart have a supple, elastic latch
that makes it easy to dispatch
all pettiness and bigotry
and opens it to what makes free?

Is the heart a huge and lovely land?
Does it know the meaning of "Expand
and make your borders bright
and luminous with love's own light"?

You who can heal all wounds and hate
make my heart open, free, and great.

Home: La Belle

To be home. To breathe the air of home.
This place of the comfortable cat,
of the bright canary.
The three of us at home and happy.
Cat and canary and Carol.
Purring.
And singing.
And breathing the air of home.

Shalom

Father Abraham, when you set out from Ur
did you feel in your seed the three great sons?
Was your body heavy with Moses' law,
with Jesus' word,
with Mohammed's surrender?

Was shalom already in your heart
when you crossed into Canaan?

When you sired two sons,
Ishmael first, then Isaac,
did you know you were bringing forth nations?
Breeding prophets?
Did Hagar intuit?
Did Sarah know?

Father Abraham, great ancestor,
Mother Sarah,
Mother Hagar,
bring your children's children's children together.
Beget now the Great Shalom.

Love's Oven

I've been in love's oven, toasted brown and crisp,
I've hung on love's tree as fruit and made succulent;
I've been nested, sat on the egg of me, warmed for the hatching,
I've been cradled and coddled and cuddled—and why?
To be oven and fruit tree and nest for the future lovers.

The Thousand Fires

Who did the deed?
Who was the heroine?
It doesn't matter.
One saves her country;
the other, a scrap of paper.
One is a martyr;
the other dies in bed.

One laughs; another cries.
It does not matter.
The one who wears a crown
wears it for all, and it sparkles
with the light from a thousand fires.

The Best Kept Secret

The best-kept secret of them all:
Here is enough.
Now is plenty.

Waiting for something else is to scorn diamonds.
Running elsewhere is to cast off pearls.

Take the jewels and adorn yourself.
You will never glow more brilliantly than here;
you will never be more radiant than now.

Remote Preparation for a Funeral

It was a moment out of time
when I first saw that aging tree
and heard its hardness call to me
and knew its roots were roots of mine.
As if somehow we knew each other,
as if somehow it were my brother.

And then I went another day.
It was all trunk and solid rose
dividing high up where it chose
in two great prongs—and who can say
which was the trunk and which the daughter?
My mind is in an awesome clutter.

And of a sudden I know why:
my father will be dead this year
the trunk that bore me's end is near,
that solidness will soon run dry.
The trunk will go and the prongs fall
and will the sap then flow at all?

Do we, too, die when fathers fade?
No, we are growing down below
in roots that have their own deep flow.
so, solidness may be betrayed.
But from below, where mothers lie,
new sap will flow when fathers die.

The First Wet Kiss

It's the nesting of birds in spring,
long hours on the shell of unknowing,
the hardness of it, the hopefulness,
knowing that finally the shell will break
and there will be the first wet kiss on the wing.

Such is the meditator
who sits on the nest of her breath
for hours and years,
sure that someday the shell of her ego will break
and her Self will take the first deep breath of life.

The Future of Community

We all come from a place of pain
and a place of peace
and the sharing is a resurrection.

It's all right to be human, hungry, hurt;
and it's all right to have joy, serenity, hope.

Trust opens our mouths to tell the truth of our pain;
trust opens our hearts to the balm of love;
trust opens our eyes to the thread of light
      that weaves us into one.

The Traveler

Homer hiding his heroes in
    the Trojan Horse,
Ulysses evading the Cyclops
    under the sheep's belly,
Virgil shepherding Aeneas
    through to Rome,
Dante scaling the Inferno,
Columbus shipping out to
    unknown shores,
Magellan on his world cruise,
Milton touring Paradise Lost,
Eliot surveying the Waste Land:
even in old age I aspire
    to such journeying.

Whoever Thinks There Is Only One God

Has never fallen silent under an oak tree,
has never worshipped water,
has never adored lilies.

Monotheism is heresy.
We live among gods.

Five Minutes in a Garden

Five minutes in a garden and you
know it's all God.
The daisies can't deceive,
the roses can't keep the secret.
We may call it a garden
but it's really the one body
the one flesh
the only life there is.

We're All Little Suns.

We're all little suns.
The chrysanthemum is a sun
unfolding light
and the soul explodes
on a stalk of green fire.
You too are a sun,
and the purple of your wisdom
is simply Lord Helios
shattering into sparks of glory.

Privilege

To think there are people who
    have never seen a squirrel,
Who spend their lives seeing only
    tigers, or polar bears, or leopards,
who have never laughed at those bushy tails,
or watched them store up acorns,
or disappear up a tree.
Perhaps it is a deprivation those
who contemplate only ostriches
    don't even know they suffer,
just as most of us will never
      know we're missing the
      tangy taste of fried worms.
It is good to remember our privilege:
not everyone sees a tiny
    fellow scamper up an oak.

Some Trees Are Gods

Some trees are gods.
You know you must bow down before them,
and ask their will.
"What would you with me, Tree?
Where should I go?
What would you have me do?"

And the tree god speaks:
"Stay here. Be silent. Listen. Take root.
And learn to know you also are a god."

Requiem

The redwood tree in the garden
turned brown suddenly. It is
being cut down today, eliminated,
disposed of, no trace left.
Tomorrow the empty space will be filled
and only a few will remember its shade,
its sturdiness, its hope.
Day after tomorrow no-one will notice.
At least today I will honor with
this requiem the gift it has been,
the sorrow we all feel.

Trees as Artists

How quaint, I thought, to draw a tree!
I don't draw trees. The trees draw me.
And I, their willing model, lie
under their gaze as they cross the sky.

They look at me with great brown eyes
and they see down there where the gizzard lies
and they take out palettes and brushes long
and they make me pose for a care-free song.

They laugh as I dance beneath their sky
and the truth they tell me is not shy:
what you lack are roots. You walk and walk
but the real sojourn's more than talk.

A pilgrim's rooted in life's brown soil
though it may mean only tears and toil.
The paradox of the pilgrim's clear:
a real rover has no fear

Of roots that run in miles of earth
as firmly planted as death—or birth.
You've a lot to learn, though your hair be gray;
fruit is born of the will to stay.

Oh, they drew me well with their brushes long—
it gave me pause in my care-free song.

Oak Tree

This morning I thanked the oak tree in our front yard
for growing wide,
for its maternal branching out,
for taking us all on,
embracing, shading,
an enormous bird that spreads its wings
and flies rootedly, spaciously,
carrying us all to that country we have heard whispers of.

Let the High Priests Die

Finally, the gods are falling away.
All of them false.
All of us idolaters.

Those poplars over there are the twelve
gates of the city;
That creek's the river of life;
that bush, the sapphire throne.

The isness of it all is what we worship,
the stripped-down-nakedness of it,
the fierce and succulent flesh of life.

Something Round

There's a Christmas ornament
all year long.
It hangs in the sky
like a poem, like a song.
it sings in the night,
it hides in the day,
it's a great white smile
that lights up the way.
It's luscious and lovely
it's shy and it's sweet,
it gives out white wisdom
and the softest white heat.
It's a mystery, it's magic,
it's a gentle white balloon.
it's a sister to the sunlight
and—you've guessed it—it's the moon.

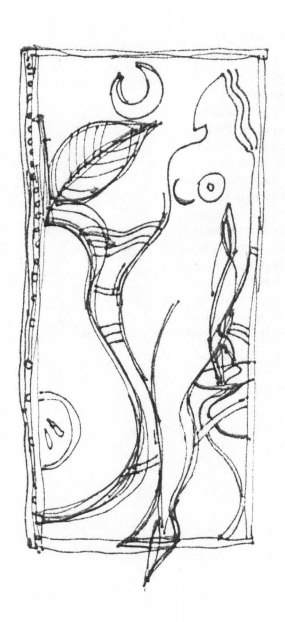

My Love Affair with the Moon

My love affair with the moon began when I was eight
and sneaked out of the house at midnight.
It was New Orleans,
and the jasmine floated, and the moon told secrets.
I stripped to my innocence and rolled on the night grass,
with my Great White Grandmother watching.
Then one night my mother missed me, scolded me, grounded me,
and the love affair was over.

So I switched allegiance.
I cleverly mastered the sun's lore
and went to his clear bright school
and learned all the right answers,
became adept at sun bathing, sun worship,
and occasionally felt a soothing sunburst in my heart.

But once in a while, laughing, a bit wistful,
I remembered that child on the grass.

Now I'm choosing moon folly once again.
I'm out on the grass at midnight under the Carmel sky,
and the Grandmother I thought was dead,
the one who taught me white magic and innocence,
my Great White Grandmother,
my Goddess,
shines down,
and we share secrets only women know.

Being Born Masculine-Gone-Crazy

It's a phallic erectness
and we're off running, running
who shall be first?

Got to be right
got to get it together
got to be right
got to do it, do it, do it now.

And more money!
Goals and victories.
Getting, achieving.
The prize in hand
and oh, when the wrapping's off
it's empty, plastic, empty.

So what happened to breast?
Where in the world is a womb?
The just being, listening, waiting,
working in the garden,
eating,
sleeping.

Until, in its own time,
without effort,
with only a going with the flow,
a baby—or is it a new world?—
is born.

The Three Ages of Morning

Morning is virgin, pristine and whole,
stepping confidently over the horizon.

Morning is mother,
in painless labor with the perfect child.

Morning is crone,
healing the darkness with a blessing of radiance.

Be Comforted

"Be comforted," she said. So I flowed with juices
and relaxed into who I've become,
fell back into comfort constantly, constantly
into comfort, the comfort of being at home
in this particular composition of cells and cartilages,
mucus and membrane. The Cancer sign of my birth
at home at last in this skeleton-walking
ecstatically-comforted-Carol-self,
feet finally on earth, with an outrageous surge of life
    within,
a hair's breadth from death and still laughing.

Love It Well

When will I be worthy to love one thing well?
Like our new home, set high
on the corner of 14th and Maple,
to be admired,
to be envied, I'm sure, by passers-by

because it's creamy white,
and there's an oak tree,
guardian spirit, in the front,
aristocratic, splendid

so clean, sweep, dust, wash, scrub, rinse, polish, shine.
Love it well!

Mary-Mirror

When Mary to her cousin went
the trees in lowly laughter bent
and luster of their greenness lent
for mirroring her merriment.

When Mary came to Calvary
it was a still and lonely tree
that stood as straight and stripped as she
for mirroring her majesty.

Follow the Flow

Knowing her first, I felt her stream run smooth,
skip playfully on rocks
and fall down liquid hills.
"Follow the flow," was her advice.
I did not understand.

In later years I met her once again.
She was a river grown,
swollen with life,
pulled by strong currents down toward unknown seas.
One felt the peaceful eddies, and the deep longing
        for the ocean's bed,
and she ran blue as the late summer years she bore.
"Follow the flow," she said.

Then there was parting, and we did not meet again
until one year when frost was chain about us.
I wondered, then, if she had frozen, too,
into the static waiting of old age,
reverting back to narrow winter stream.
But when I saw her eyes, I knew
she was Pacific now, and stretched horizons and
        beyond.
Ice could not crust on her
nor the frost chain
but rather wisdom pulled her tides.
Her deeps were heavy with the weight of love.

I understood, then, what it is to follow flow:
someday, one meets and mingles with the sea.

Song for an Old Woman

It is not my fault that I am holy.
It's all God's doing.
When I wasn't looking he tricked me onto the path,
knocked me off balance
so that I gasped for help,
and threw me onto my knees.
How could I help it that I landed
on Paradise Road?

Apollo in the Decade of the Sixties

Something about the shining of Apollo
something about the Muse.

Something about a steadfast sun,
the unbreakable light,
the direct gaze,
the different kind of tenderness.

His steadiness wedded to softness,
the firm hand on my breasts.

The certainty that milk will flow from them,
even now, under his serene touch,
in the fullness of my elder years.

The Question

So, since I live on, shall my moments be
as the exuberant flame,
a sudden conflagration of bone and soul
that makes the winter solstice merry?

Or do I need smoldering ash,
the steady burning of days and years
that heats, not one ecstatic room,
but the whole house of life?

The Wind

The wind asks for nothing—
it sweeps in,
sweeps clean,
empties,
frees.

God, you are wind
and an always new beginning.

Close to the Last

Close to the last
but no death rattle yet,
I decide to finger a trumpet
announcing as ostentatiously as possible
that life has been quite an adventure,
and I fully expect there to be
endless encores.

A Seven's Farewell

(The 7 on the Enneagram is "the happy one")

So when I say goodbye, let it be heartfelt.
Wave a kiss to the world on the way out.
It's been good.
Hopefully, there will be a farewell party
and rich red wine.
Maybe a shower,
with gifts for the next world.
Maybe best wishes
for the next incarnation.

Whatever.

At that moment I'll just be curious.
Curious, but not afraid.
Oh yes, I have my own little list of peccadillos.
Perhaps I should have some anxiety,
but, strangely, I don't.

I'm just longing to see the face
of that persistent love,
of the amazing one
who's made all this fun possible.

After All This Comfort

So, after all this comfort,
you think you will die uncomforted?
Ludicrous!
Blasphemy!

You will die hugged to the breast,
nursed into light.
It will be the deepest comfort, and you
will celebrate wedding.
You will stand at the altar in that final
caressing and say "Amen!" to the great questioning.
You who said "Yes" will keep repeating
"Yes, indeed yes!"

And there will be a comfortable,
an infinitely comforting
Beginning Kiss.

At the End

The same labor pains
that erupted you into life set in.
The moment to push hasn't come yet:
only the pain and the trust
and the imploding of unknown worlds.

Last Word

Last word before sleep:
enough,
bread and water
blessings upon blessings.

The Tao of Now, nothing else.
What is enough for breathing
for belonging here,
holding the pulse of the present,
enough for survival,
a spoiled guest of today upon the planet.
I do believe it was enough,
enough food
enough drink,
and enough to share with a friend.

Dying: a Pagan View

Dying is not delicious—
it's devilish hard,
though the Divine is not far off.
In fact, it is rather dramatic
drastic, to say the least,
and decidedly definitive,
and may drag on for days
or deftly dispose of us in minutes.
Anyway,
death is deadly
and will come when it damned pleases.

Pioneer

Know when to embrace that strangest of ecstasies,
    death.

Walk fearlessly into uncharted territory.
You have always been a pioneer.

Be the explorer now
as you stand on the rim.

Amateur midwife that I am,
I have seen birth three times,
and I swear that one popped out with an enormous
    smile.

Even so, let go smiling into that last embrace.

May My Ashes

May my ashes
leap in the froth of the ocean
still ready to dance for the world.

First Line Index

G

H

I

I've been in love's oven, toasted brown and crisp (92)
I will not let the angel of joy (50)
I will stand on the busiest corner of Manhattan (37)

K

Knowing her first, I felt her stream run smooth (117)
Know when to embrace that strangest of ecstasies, death (128)

L

Last word before sleep (126)
Let the small gods die (23)

M

May my ashes (129)
Mine was a quiet house, carefully constructed (48–49)
Morning is virgin, pristine and whole (113)
My love affair with the moon began when I was eight (111)
My way makes a trail in the water (22)

N

Nothing is more like God than the ocean (69)
Now I need travel no more (24)

O

On Buddha's birthday, how do you celebrate? (18)
Once upon a see-saw moment (61)

P

Perhaps all that's left is to know (63)
Poetry divides my life in phases (38)

S

Sanity is not the way (58)
Seven years you have pounded my shore (66)
Shall I tell you about the golden woman
       who danced in my dream? (73)
She said she swims in God (77)
She sits in front of the TV at the Family Justice Center (71)
Since the voice of my soul spoke out (43)
So, after all this comfort (124)
So everything is radiance (55)
So let words tumble out as they will (45)
Something about the shining of Apollo (119)
Some trees are gods (104)
So, since I live on, shall my moments be (120)
So what is the finding of a friend (78)
So when I say goodbye, let it be heartfelt (123)
Suddenly I knew (84)

T

That map of happiness you gave me (57)
The best-kept secret of them all (94)
The Hindus knew it (83)
The redwood tree in the garden (105)
There's a Christmas ornament (109)
There's no such thing as future tense (53)
The same labor pains (125)
The wind asks for nothing (121)
The woman in me, lake-like, looks to the mountain (85)
This is a poem about the body (36)
This morning I thanked the oak tree in our front yard (107)
Though my feet are too old to whirl (35)

To be home. To breathe the air of home (90)
Today I was a little more deliberate (31)
To think there are people who (102)

W

We all come from a place of pain (97)
We breathe their bones (87)
We're all little suns (101)
We start alone. Uniqueness draws its breath (81)
What Chagall did with his painting (47)
What is is enough (80)
What jolts me alive is a voice (41)
When I come to you for pardon (27)
When I'm called in to mourn with you (75)
When I stand by the sea (39)
When Mary to her cousin went (116)
When will I be worthy to love one thing well? (115)
"When you give a banquet" (72)
When you speak I hear you (30)
Where is humility? (64)
Who did the deed? (93)

Y

You've loved me in many ways, my God (32)

CPSIA information can be obtained
at www.ICGtesting.com
Printed in the USA
LVHW031549230520
656343LV00006B/472